MONOLOGUES THEY HAVEN'T HEARD

Roger Karshner

Dramaline Publications

Dramaline® Publications
36-851 Palm View Road
Rancho Mirage, CA 92270
Phone: 760-770-6076 Fax: 760-770-4507
Web site: dramaline.com Email: drama.line@verizon.com

Library of Congress Cataloging-in-Publication Data

Karshner, Roger.
    Monologues They Haven't Heard / Roger Karshner
        p. cm.
    ISBN 0-9611792-01 (alk. paper): $9.95
    1. Monologues. I. Title.
PS3561. A695M66   1994
812' .54—dc20

Cover design, John Sabel

This book is printed on 55# Glatfelter acid-free paper. A paper that meets the requirements of the American Standard of Permanence of paper for printed library material.

CONTENTS

WOMEN: COMEDY

AVA

During a brief bar encounter, Ava learns that it's not wise to be overly revealing to strangers.

(*Responding to a question.*) Where do I work? I work over at Hillcrest. You know, the cemetery? The big one over on the east side that's loaded with ornate fountains and statues. We call it "Valhalla With Smog." (*A pause for listening.*)

Death gives you the creeps? Well, that's normal, I guess. I mean, nobody really *likes* it. Unless they're some kind of sicko, or something. (*Pause.*) I'm in sales over there. A good job. (*A pause for listening.*)

Recession-proof? No way. I wish it were. But when business is off, it's off everywhere. Oh, I don't mean people stop dying. Hardly. What happens is, they cheap-out on the funerals. Instead of roses, they go for violets and they cut back on the caskets. But even when things are off, I do pretty well because we always have clients. Last month I made close to three thousand dollars. One heck of a month. I work on a draw against commission. And I get good benefits. We try to get people to speculate, to make pre-arrangements. We call it "Future Planning." Kind of a contradiction in terms, really, isn't it? An oxymoron. I mean—where's the future, right?

We avoid terms like "death" and "dying." Instead, we use expressions like "The Eternal Sleep," "The Royal Beginning." Nice, easy, little flowery expressions that make it easier on the customer. We do our best to minimize the grief, you know. My boss makes up the slogans. He used to be a big deal in advertising. He's also the president of Hillcrest. We're a major corporation. Big business.

One of the biggest problems facing our business is the shortage of land. We take options on dump sites. When we can, we try to bury 'em double-decker. It saves twice the space. We give a special deal on bunk beds. A lot of people won't go for it, though. They don't like the thought of themselves or their loved ones being on the bottom.

One of our salesmen sold a family on a mausoleum last week. He made over five thousand commission. The guy's a fantastic closer. He's already gone over a million dollars in sales this year. He was awarded this little gold casket to wear in his lapel. (*A pause for response.*) Another stinger? Sure, why not. (*Pause.*) By the way, what do you do? (*A pause for response.*) A writer? Hey, that's interesting. What are you working on? (*Pause for response.*) An exposé of the funeral business? (*She slaps her drink to the bar and rises.*) See you 'round, sport.

BETTY

Betty expresses her disillusionment with men in general.

No way. Forget it, Jan. Can't you get it through your head that I can't stand Harry? Harry is past-tense. Harry is history. You have no idea what a dick he is. You only see the one side of him; the cutesy, phony side that says, "Lookie, lookie, I'm a nice little cookie." Well, he's not. He's a jerk.

You know, it's getting more and more difficult every day to meet a nice, regular, down-to-earth guy. One without hangups and problems. And you can't go by looks, either. God, no. About a month ago, I met this really great-looking guy, okay? Who drove a new four-wheeler, wore faded Levis, plaid shirts, boots. Paul Bunyan, right? Wrong. Turns out he was gay. Like I said, you just can't tell in this crazy, upside-down world of ours, anymore. Maybe it's just me, I don't know. Maybe there's something about me that attracts losers. (*She reflects.*) Maybe a nunnery's the answer. Maybe those women have the right idea: abstinence, celibacy, and all that. I've got a good notion to check it out. "Sister Betty Bowers." Doesn't have a bad ring to it, does it? (*Pause.*) I've had it with men for a while. I think I'll give romance a rest. (*She does a quick over-the-shoulder take.*) Jan, don't turn around! But when you go to the restroom, check out the guy in the leather jacket at the bar. What a hunk!

LISA

Lisa employs irony as a means of making her point with her profligate mother.

Sure, Mother, sure, it's just great being broke. Wonderful. It's super. Poverty is delightful. Nothing like living on the edge without gas and electricity. It'll be neat being primitive. We can forage for food and make our own clothing. Hey, I can't wait. And I'm sure *you'll* love it, too. *S-u-u-u-r-e* you will.

It'll be an exciting new lifestyle for you. No more Gucci-Pucci. No more shows. No trips to Europe. No more daily martini klatches at the Plaza. No more summers in the Hamptons. But who needs all that, right? Not you, n-o-o-o-o-o. Oh no—you're independent now. This is the life. Being flat is where it's at.

I think it was just brilliant not to save a dime and to spend like crazy. I mean, after all, what's money for, anyway? Like the thirty thousand you blew on the Halloween party. Cute. You could have been a little prudent, invested, planned a little. But, what the hell, we were "in," we were "happening," we "got down." We got down, all right. So far down that now we're down and out. But that's okay, that's cool.

This is going to be the *real* life. It'll be great not having a car. Walking's one of the healthiest things a person can do. Next summer, we can walk up to the Hamptons and check out the garbage. And you can walk to the welfare office. And I'm sure you're going to love working. I hear there's a real glamour position open at Kmart making keys.

Yes, Mommie dear, this is going to be a wonderful, beautiful adventure. Hey, we can look on it as a test to see if we can make it below the poverty level. Just think of the advantages. Now we'll be able to get next to street people and the homeless and hobnob with the lower crust. Just think of it, big spender. Isn't the thought of being poor exciting?

Never work with animals or children.
—Anonymous (a show business maxim)

MRS. CARTWRIGHT

Mrs. Cartwright warns against the use of "demon" stimulants.

Stimulants! No good! Bad for ya! Coke, coffee, tea—any of it! Why, the amount a caffeine in that stuff makes people crazy.

Like this one fella in the community, Dwayne Myers. He had a swell family, a nice little wife, was knockin' down big money. But then he went and let that devil Pepsi Cola getta hold on him. He went off in all directions, just like some wildman. Lost 'is religion, gave up a dandy job. The last we heard, he was a-livin' over in Grand Fork with some snip of a girl half 'is age.

Stimulants! Even your decaf, you can't trust that, either. You know, I understand there's hippies in the factories slippin' caffeine into the Sanka. Them long-haired weirdos'll go to any lengths. If Nixon was still president, they wouldn't be gettin' away with it. Dick Nixon never took no stimulants, you can bet yer sweet life on it. And stimulants can cause bad constipation, too. Cyrus Henry usta drink a coupla pots a coffee a day, and he wound up with an impacted bowel. He swelled up like a toad. His wife, the poor little thing, she thought he was gonna go an' bust on 'er. Caffeine wrecked his health. He usta be a big, strappin' man. Now he looks like a pygmy. Constipation. One of the worst things that can ever happen to a person. That an' bad feet.

SHERRIE

Sherrie, a loquacious small-town girl, rambles on.

You own a town? Like a whole town, really? Wow! I've never known anyone who owned their own town before. Well, I did know this one guy back home who owned a mobile-home park. Just for old people. You had to be over seventy to live there. He

said that dying was good for business. Turnover, you know. He wasn't a very nice person. He was a real creep, that guy. He was forever trying to get me into bed. "Look," I'd tell him, "I'm not that kind of girl." I'm from Wheeling, West Virginia. The Mountain State. But we don't really have mountains, though. More like hills. Not much is happening back there, but it's real pretty. Every spring, we get floods. They wash out everything. One time a house was washed all the way down to Parkersburg. A very destructive thing, floods. Hey, when nature lets go—forget it. That's the reason I believe in God. Some people don't, you know. But I think it's good to have God on your side. 'Specially when you're traveling across the country alone like I am. You never know what might happen at some rest stop. Men. A girl can't be too careful. I like men, though. I went steady with this one guy all through high school. His name was Doyle. He was this short little guy, but he was real strong. We almost had to get married because I thought I was pregnant. Thank God I wasn't, 'cause Doyle was a mess.

BERNICE

Bernice, a compulsive overeater, agonizes and speaks of her commitment to overcome.

I've tried every diet known to man: Slim Fast, Weight Watchers, Nutri-System, Jenny Craig—you name it. Hell, I'd chew on plywood if I thought it would work.

Most people have no idea how overweight I really am because I always wear loose-fitting, full-length dresses to cover it up. God, if they only knew what was going on underneath. Thank heavens for the man who invented the muu-muu. As far as I'm concerned, he should be placed right up there with Jonas Salk, should get the Nobel Prize for coming up with a cure for terminal waistline. My hero—Dr. Melvin Muu-Muu.

And now, on top of everything, right in the middle of my new diet, the holidays are just around the corner. I could die. All of those tempting cookies and cakes and chocolates lit by glorious candlelight. I'm not accepting invitations. No way. I'm not answering the phone or opening my mail till after the holidays.

Overeating's a curse. Nobody with a normal appetite knows how awful it is being plagued by it; what it's like to be wakened up in the middle of the night by a Twinkie nightmare.

God, to have anorexia for even a day; to not have a nagging appetite; to be able to get on a scale without the meter spinning; to be able to slip into a stylish dress for a change instead of a basic black parachute; to be able to survive just one day without a sugar rush; to not get hit on by only fat men. What I wouldn't give. Eyeteeth. Anything!

It's a fight. Every day it's a battle. And I'm fighting. You're damned right, I am. I'm in there slugging. I swear, I'll beat the blubber if I have to Crazy Glue my lips together.

Pray to God and say the lines.

—Bette Davis (Ruth Elizabeth Davis; 1908–1989), advice to Celeste Holm

ADRIENNE

She admonishes her ex-lover for fantasizing that marrying a virgin will be a panacea.

Bill, who do you think you're talking to here? Listen to me. I know you like Seattle knows rain. And you're kidding yourself. You haven't got a chance in hell of making it with Mary Beth. Just how long do you think you'll be happy with a school-marm? With buttons and bows and a bright golden haze on your meadow?

Mary Beth isn't real, Bill. She's freeze-dried. She's sweepers and recipes and *Family Circle*. She'll make her own dresses and force you to eat fried chicken five nights a week. And on your honeymoon—you can bet on it—she'll insist on seeing Disney World.

Don't you see, virgin-breath, that this is all wrong? And that's another thing—she's a virgin. You're out of your mind to marry a girl who's never been road-tested. Anyway, I still don't believe it. Still a virgin at twenty-five? C'mon. Where the hell's she been for a quarter-century, anyway? Frozen in a block of ice someplace like the Frankenstein monster, or something?

And just think about your wedding night.*Think* about it. If it turns out she really *is* a virgin, that is. God—it'll be like touching wet paint. You'd better call off this stupid wedding while you've still got a chance. Before you wake up some

morning and find yourself in a Motel 6 in N
bed full of forbidden fruit.

(*A pause for his response.*) What? Me jealous? *Me?* ᴎ.
kidding? C'mon, get real. I'm just thinking about you here,
that's all. Hey, I know you like a book, Bill, face it. (*A pause
for his response.*) I said I'm not jealous—okay? I mean—
anyway, why should I be? I mean, after all it's, it's. . . . (*Then,
quickly.*) Okay, okay, all right—I'm jealous, I'm jealous! I
mean, what do you expect? I'm bound to feel *something.* After
all, five years living together is a long haul.

Just know your lines and don't bump into the furniture.
—Noel Coward (1899–1973, British Dramatist, advice to actors

DIANE

Diane's self-respect supersedes her career.

Look, friend, let me give you a little quick history: I came out here a little over two years ago. I hitched out, as a matter of fact, with this tattooed pervert in a rusted-out RV who tried his damndest to get me into the back of the thing for over two-thousand miles. But I didn't cave in. And I haven't caved in since I've been here, in spite of hearing every proposition from some of the biggest of the big-time scumbags.

I came out here with the intention of making it in the business because I think I have some talent. If I don't, after a fair shot, it's back to Dayton and a job at GE.

I may not be working right now, may not be "up for a series," but I'm also not up for *you!* Not now, not ever. If I make it, whatever "making it" is—and I'm beginning to wonder altogether—I'll make it on my feet, not horizontal.

(*Throwing down a script with a gesture of finality.*) So, here's your script. Enjoy it. Frankly, I didn't. I really can't get into a hooker who does a heart patient in the rear of an ambulance. I wouldn't do it in the back of an RV for a ride, and I won't do it in the back of ambulance for scale. See you 'round, film person. (*She EXITS.*)

SALLY

Sally's anxiety grows commensurate with the approaching hour of her dental appointment.

(*Indicating her underarms.*) Look. Get a load of the perspiration rings! (*Pause for response.*) Yes, you're right, I'm afraid of the dentist. No, "afraid" isn't the word. "Terrified" is the word. (*Pause for response.*) I know, I know that. I know they've got all kinds of modern equipment. But that still doesn't alter the fact that I'm scared to death of dentists.

I've been this way ever since I was a little girl. Ever since Dr. Cross, my first dentist. He had this little dingy office over a Rexall drug store. One flight up. A walkup. You know, I can still see that long flight of stairs leading up to his torture chamber. It always was like walking the last mile. What a memory. (*She shivers at the recollection.*)

And you should have seen Dr. Cross: a little bald-headed creep with big forceps. And rotten teeth. (*A pause for response.*) No, I swear, the guy looked like a bad-breath commercial. The only thing I can figure is that he was afraid to go to the dentist. A smart man, Dr. Cross. And he was a real ogre, this guy. He had this mad-scientist look in his eyes. And he just loved pain—other people's. Dr. Cross was a real agony vendor.

When I had a toothache, I'd never let on that it hurt. Not until the pain became unbearable and my cheek blew up like a purple meatball. That's how much I hated going.

My father was the one who always took me because my mother couldn't stand the sight of her only child being tortured. I never slept a wink the night before. And by the time of the appointment, I'd be a nervous wreck—sick inside. And right before we got to Dr. Cross' office, the pain would always mysteriously subside, and I'd tell my dad I was okay and that we should go on back home. But it never worked.

Dr. Cross's waiting room was painted this bilious shade of green, and it smelled like the inside of a medicine cabinet. His nurse's name was Mrs. Sweet. She was very masculine and super fat, and when she walked, her legs rubbed together and made a swishing sound. When it was my turn, Dad and Mrs. Sweet had to drag me into the dental chair, screaming. One time I kicked Dr. Cross and broke the gold chain that held his elk's tooth. (*Noting her underarms.*)

God, look! Get a load of the perspiration rings now. It's like my armpits are leaking. By the time of my appointment, they'll be all the way down to my waist. What time is it, anyway? (*Pause for response.*) What? Already? Oh, Jesus!

JUDY

Recently divorced, Judy ruminates regarding her marriage while preparing to paint a room.

(*Noting a wall.*) Well, how's it look? (*Pause for response.*) You think? (*A pause for response.*) Well, professional or not, I'm not about to go dropping a bundle on painters. I'm doing it myself. Besides, I'm suspicious of painters. I mean, you never know if they're wearing anything under their coveralls. (*A pause for response.*)

Ask Harry? Are you kidding? I wouldn't ask Harry for lint. Besides, it's not his problem anymore.

Good old Harry. He just couldn't handle it because I wouldn't become his full-time servant. Couldn't hack it because I wouldn't be his housekeeper. All I ever was to him was a nut-bread baker, his helpmate, the little woman, the squaw, the better half—the *slave!* I did my damnedest, but I just couldn't fill the role of his mother. And I tried. God, did I ever. Do you realize that for seven years I was nothing more than room service in this vine-covered Hilton?

If he'd bent even a little bit, given me even an ounce of independence. But, oh no, he wanted me here at the ranch doing chores. He had these very old-fashioned, ingrained, macho ideas about the roles of husbands and wives. Harry was like a lot of men still are, Doris. He was a frontier husband. I guess it was a carryover from his childhood environment. His mother does everything but bring his dad the paper in her teeth.

I hung in as long as I could. But being subservient and baking brownies for life isn't my deal. After a while, as hard as I tried, I just couldn't handle it anymore. I was starting to feel like one of Jane Austin's characters..

I have to admit, I do miss the pampered little cowboy every now and then, though. I mean, he wasn't all bad. But, basically, he was still part of the Old West. You know what he actually said to me the day I told him he had to move out? Are you ready for this? He said I'd ambushed him before he'd had time to get his wagons in a circle. He actually said that.

Hand me that roller coater, will you, Doris.

Ladies, a little more virginity, if you don't mind.

—Herbert Beerbohm Tree (1853–1917), British actor and
theater manager while directing a group of sophisticated actresses

WOMEN: DRAMA

MARTHA

Martha, never close to her father, recalls a fleeting, rare tender moment in their relationship.

Father, father, dear father.

He never had time for us; any of us, ever. Even for mother; not even for her. She was nothing more than his housekeeper. I never saw him offer her an ounce of affection, ever. He related to her with cool, offhanded professionalism. I've often felt that her death meant nothing more to him than inconvenience.

As a child, I remember him as an elegant vagrant, coming and going in his mannered, indifferent way; a transient who had neither time or inclination for his family. He never had time, especially for me, the youngest. Only once. . . .

Yes, there was this one moment. I was quite young, I remember. Very young, in fact. And it was summer. And I was playing by the wisteria. (*Remembering.*) Yes, by the wisteria. (*She points OFF.*) Over there where the arbor used to be. Suddenly, I felt a large, warm, hovering presence as if the sun were at my shoulder. I looked up, and there was father, standing there above me, watching me in silence. Then, unexpectedly and uncharacteristically, he reached down and stroked my hair—ever so gently he stroked it. (*She fingers her hair with an expression of wistfulness at the memory.*)

His hand moved lightly, in and out of my tresses. And his eyes, I particularly remember his eyes, because for once they didn't seem to have that glasslike quality that deflected penetration. For that moment, they seemed warm and receptive.

And, for that moment, for what seemed a fleeting lifetime, I felt safe, and secure—and loved.

Nothing to be fixed except your performance.

—Noel Coward, replying to a telegram from
Gertrude Lawrence—"Nothing wrong that can't be fixed"—
refering to her part in Coward's play *Private Lives*

SARAH

Sarah, a country girl, describes how, through her father, she came to understand the special quality that had existed between him and her recently deceased mother.

We drove on out to the grave last Sunday, Dad and I. And it was rainin' a fine-lace drizzle. I'd never ever seen the place quite like that before; so quiet and fresh and green. In fact, I'd never seen a lot of things, or felt 'em like I did last Sunday. And I felt what Dad was feelin'. Yes, I did. It was almost like—like I was inside 'is body.

It was beautiful the way he walked up there; the way he walked up to the grave real light like, like he didn't want to intrude. And when he reached the grave, he just stood there, lookin' down at it like he was a-lookin' right on through the earth, right into the soul o' Mother.

And then, right then and there, for the very first time, I realized what they'd had between 'em. It was that they'd loved each other with a love that only a few people ever know; a deep love that connects 'em even now, even now that she's away. I always knew they cared a lot for each other, but I never felt it like this when she was alive. But here now, at her grave, alluva sudden, I was part of their world.

KRISTIN

Kristin, a now-penniless heiress, unleashes her ire on her ne'er-do-well husband.

You know what I say? I say shame and pity on the whole god-damned human race for treating its people like dirt, like fucking tramps! What the hell ever happened to compassion, anyway? What the hell ever happened to that? I'll tell you what: it was bought off like everything else, that's what. Compassion and feeling and caring and understanding—all down the drain for money and power.

And you, why hell, you're just like all the rest. With you it's the same—money and power. You—why, you're nothing but a weak, money-grubbing little bastard who ran out of love when the money ran out! And you have the balls, the audacity to stand there and talk about our relationship. Relationship, hell! Our relationship was nothing but trusts and stocks and dollars and bonds and who held the key to the safe-deposit box. Well, now all that's gone! And I'm glad. Glad because now that the money's stripped away, you're naked and I can see the real you and see into that little distorted mind of yours; a mind like the ones behind the business of business that cheats and connives and wrangles and sells out and corrupts. I know you. I know a thousand yous. And none of you are worth a bloody shit!

JANET

Janet lectures Lloyd, a recent widower. She criticizes him for living in the past and for not accepting the present and for not looking to the future without guarantees.

Why not just go ahead and enjoy your life? Live it day to day. What's wrong with that? Look at Sally. She's your age and you don't find her sitting around on her butt, complaining, bitching, waiting for Mr. Wonderful.

And as for me marrying you—forget it. You're a sweet guy and I care for you a lot, but I like my life just the way it is, thank you. I'm not interested in complications. I'm a businesswoman and I have my independence and I love it and I wouldn't change a thing for the world.

Besides, you don't want to marry me, Lloyd—not really. You want to marry the past and pretend that things are the same as they always were with Mary because you can't let go of yesterday. You want to remarry because you're scared to death of facing life without someone to lean on because that's how it's always been. You're selling out all of your options because you're afraid to face up and bite the bullet and make a real effort to change and get on with it.

Mary's gone, face up to it! She's dead, Lloyd—dead! It's a sad fact, but that's the way it is, and you can't change it by rejecting the reality of it and hiding behind yesterday. You can't bury yourself with her and keep running from the present. I know it's one hell of a cliché, but hell, man—life goes on.

Why can't you just enjoy a nice relationship with a woman without guarantees? And another thing: one of the reasons your daughter keeps babying you is because you really haven't made an honest effort to cut that off, either. You need Julie over here every five minutes, kissing your ego and reminding you of your past. For Christ's sake, Lloyd, quit viewing life in the rear-view mirror and start looking on down the road.

I'm a wife-made man.

—Danny Kaye

(his wife Sylvia Fine wrote most of his best lyrics)

MEN: COMEDY

MICHAEL

Michael delivers an impassioned speech regarding the dangers of total honesty.

Hey, hey, just a minute here, now. I mean—that much honesty is stupid, okay? And besides, it's wrong. All of this nonsense about spilling your guts, about getting everything out in the open, "telling it like it is," is bullshit. Telling it like it is is usually an excuse for people to unload all their backed-up poison. Hey! Listen to me,here, okay? Are you listening?

Tell me what the hell ever happened to discretion and restraint. What the hell ever happened to respecting the feelings of others? Don't get me wrong, now. I don't mean we should go around lying all the time, but there are ways of laying the truth on people without loading it into a gun and blowing their brains out with it. Understand? Are you listening to me here? Some people get heavy into therapy and that and then they run around with a goddamned couch on their back like psychiatric assholes. Know what I mean?

Okay, now, listen. Are you listening to me? The way I look at it, see, is that you can get said what you want without psychic diarrhea. And, besides, total honesty gets a lot of poor jerks into very big trouble. Like my dad had a thing going with our cleaning lady for years, okay? For years she came in every Monday to do the laundry and my old man. But you think my old man went blabbing to my mother, "Edith, every Monday while you're at the hospital rolling bandages, I'm rolling

Marie?" Hey! My old man was no idiot. No way. He knew the importance of discretion, you know.

So, you gotta be careful how much you tell Ida. You go spilling the details about your ex-ladies, and you and Ida become history, okay? Then you're back to being a bachelor and playing with yourself and eating TV dinners. So, no matter how hard she pumps—pump, pump, pump—and they can pump, baby, they can pump. No matter how hard she pumps, you don't tell her shit, okay?

You're a virgin, remember? You're cherry. Are you listening to me here?

It is easier to get an actor to be a cowboy than to get a cowboy to be an actor.

—John Ford (Sean O'Feeney; 1895–1973), U.S. film director

LARRY

Larry, an ex-jock, unashamedly reveals his homosexuality.

Yes, that's right, Billy boy, you heard right—I'm gay. I came out over two years ago. The tendency was always there—underlying, you know. And it all came rushing forth when I met Rodney. We met in an antique shop, where I noticed him staring at me over this lovely Early American quilt. There was an instant attraction.

This is the greatest thing that's ever happened to me. Now, finally, thank heavens, I'm comfortable with my sexuality. Now I'm finally over all the sports silliness: football and all that tackling and kicking and running and sweating and ugliness. Sports. Such a waste for a person with untapped creative talents.

Now I'm heavy into interior decoration. And I'm an absolute whiz, too. While I'm here, I'll be happy to redo, if you like. (*Observing the room critically.*) Frankly, Billy, your place is rather drab. I suggest your earth tones: your browns, your soft greens, your golds, your russets, your basic autumn shades. And, oh yes—your bittersweets, definitely your bittersweets.

I'll say one thing for you, though, you keep the place neat as a pin. You must keep it covered with Saran wrap. But the furnishings? Oh my. Yuckie-wuckie, Billy boy, yuckie-wuckie. I suggest our moderns mixed tastefully with your antiques and your plants. Oh yes, your plants! Let them run wild, let them take over. Plants, plants, plants! I'm terrific with plants. I have quite a flair for casual greenery.

Rodney is *fab*ulous, you'll just love him. He's opened me up to so many things. My horizons are expanding like crazy. I'm heavy into Zen. With Shinto Goldberg. He was a rabbi who swung over. He's just *fab*ulous. You'll just love him. He's the author of *The Deli Way to Meditation*. It has to do with corned beef's influence upon Buddha.

Oh, darling, this is going to be such a fun visit. I'm just dying to meet your fiancée. If you like her, she just has to be *fab*ulous.

Speak the speech, I pray you, as I pronounced it to you, trippingly on the tongue. . . .

—William Shakespeare (1564–1616)

RANDY

Why would any woman reject Randy? After all, he's such a "class guy."

I musta asked her a hundred times. But every time she puts me down and makes me feel like shit. So, what the hell's the point? I mean, how many times can a dude get kicked in the balls by some broad, you know. These here California bimbos are a buncha goddamned snobs, man, a buncha assholes all trying to break into show biz. What's a regular guy like me gonna say to 'em? I mean, I don't know doodly shit about Shakespeare. I mean, what the fuck, man!

Last week, me and Eddie go down to Palm Springs, okay? There was broads all over living hell down there, man. You've never seen so much ass in your life. And they hang out and drink and bullshit in these outfits that are like spray-painted on, you know. But like just try an' put a move on 'em. Hey, it's like you got B.O. or something, understand? I mean, c'mon!

I don't get it. I guess it's like Eddie says: "A lotta chicks today are fulla shit." And like Eddie knows what's happening, man, 'cause this dude's been someplace; he's a hip guy. Like he says: "When you're dealing with bimbos with their heads up their ass, you ain't got a chance."

It's real hard to figure, you know. Maybe it's me. But hey! I mean, like, after all, I ain't bad looking. And I been around. And I got bucks on me. I think it's just this ball-buster attitude that a lotta women have nowadays. They get off on making a guy feel like he's wearing dirty shorts. It's no wonder a lotta guys go for hookers. I mean, hey, a man's gotta have some release, you know. He's gotta get himself some self-respect somehow. I mean, how many times can a guy get shot outta the saddle by some slut who thinks her butt's made outta china?

It's real hard to figure. I guess broads these days just ain't interested in class guys like me.

Can't act, can't sing, slightly bald.
Can dance a little.

—Anonymous. Report on Fred Astaire's first screen test.

LITTLE STICKS

Little Sticks has stumbled onto two million dollars worth of cocaine. In this speech, he speaks enthusiastically of liberation and fantasizes about his future.

Now I can travel. Now I can travel my buns off. Gulliver never traveled like I'm gonna travel, man—Marco Polo, nobody. I'm going to be a regular Rand McNally. Living in the shadow of bebop is about to come to an end. No more hearing about *swing* and *jazz* and *licks* and shit like that; no more having to hear scratchy seventy-eights and scat vocals; no more hip chicks and cool cats and far-out horseshit about Prez and Sarah. This is the end of "Little Sticks," a nobody retail flunky nudnick numb-nuts, and the birth of Harold Miller—Esquire, Playboy, womanizer, hotshot jet-set baby in tailored suits with the latest lapels and shoes and socks that match. All thanks to two million bucks worth of falling-down fucking snitz! All on account of two million beautiful bucks' worth of blowzine! Marching powder. (*He marches in place.*) Right-left-right-left, hup-one-two-three, hup-one-two-three. (*He stops his marching.*) Two million bucks worth of pure mother cocaine! It'll be the perfect coke caper. This bit will go down in the annals of big-time stories. Yeah. And when I'm old and screwed out and all wrinkled up from too much sun from lying around beaches like a dried-up jet-set grape, I'll have my beautiful twelve-year-old nympho mistress write it all down and mail it into the *New York Times* from Brazil.

FRANK

Frank can't get in sync with the athletic demands of his female contemporaries.

Then, alluva sudden, she says (*In a high-pitched, feminine voice.*), "Do you ski?" And, naturally, I say, "Sure." I mean, you think I'm going to admit to being an uncoordinated klutz? And anyway, I figured she'd forget all about it after a couple more glasses of moderately priced vino. But no such luck, babe. Later she says,(*In the high-pitched, feminine voice.*), "How about this weekend?" So, here I am trapped, right? Trapped into driving three hundred miles and spending a fortune and freezing my buns off and making a fool of myself and maybe breaking every bone in my body. So what I did was, I call her up and (*With a gravely voice.*) fake laryngitis (*Normal voice.*) and get out of it.

I don't get it, Ralph, it's crazy. How women are into all this sports stuff, I mean. They're becoming more macho than men. And the bodies on 'em anymore. Hey, check it out. Their wrists are becoming thicker with each passing generation. You should have seen the size of the forearms on the lady I dated last weekend. The chick looked like Popeye.

What ever happened to the nice, old-fashioned girl who liked to catch a flick, have a couple of beers and a burger, and then fuck your brains out? They just aren't around anymore. Another beautiful American element shot to hell. Vanished. Like a good cigar, the five-cent candy bar—the buffalo.

And how about women who are into weight training? Can you believe this? Huh? I'm asking you here, Ralph, can you believe it? Why, you ever date a lady weight-lifter and she'll wind up cleaning and jerking you for sure. Very unhealthy stuff going down in our society today, Ralph, very unhealthy. Unnatural. The women are becoming men and the men are becoming wimps. A very scary trend—very scary.

Can you picture your grandmother running in a 10K? Croquet, that was their sport; a nice genteel game in nice feminine dresses with tea-cakes and a little lemonade on the side. Women back then were an altogether different breed of cat. Today—today they're just strange pussy.

The art of acting consists of keeping people from coughing.

—Ralph Richardson (1902–1983)

WALTER

Walter laments being unemployed.

My mother would always say to me, "Walter," she would say, "think of your future. Don't wind up like your father, get into something solid." My father was—I guess you might call him a dreamer, an idea man. He had an idea for everything except for how to pay the bills. Some men were now and then between jobs. My dad was always between ideas. Once in a while, he'd stumble onto something and we'd have money for a few days and he'd buy us all kinds of stuff and take us on trips. The finest hotels. While the money lasted, nothing was too good. But most of the time we were broke, and we'd hide in the pantry when bill collectors came so they wouldn't think we were home. Have you any idea what it's like hunching in a closet with your mom and dad and playing Parcheesi by flashlight?

So, I figured engineering was the way to go, that there'd always be a job for an engineer, right? So, I prepared, went to college, did all the numbers. The day I got fired, I couldn't believe it. And they didn't fire me, oh no, they "phased me out." Phased me out! When they told me it was over, that I was history, I was mentally zapped. I couldn't talk, couldn't move. I just sat there staring at my boss's executive yo-yo. Afterwards, I went straight to the men's room and threw up in the sink. (*Beat.*) So much for security.

PETER

Peter tells of his retaliation for rude audition treatment.

So, I go to the studio and read for this guy and he nods and whispers to this other guy who was wearing director clothes. You know—chinos, a blue oxford cloth, button-down shirt, tennies, and one of those stupid little rain hats. Then this director-type person whispers something to the other guy and gets up and leaves the room. After a while, he comes back with this real tall woman with a skinny face and mousey hair and these stupid, oversize glasses. She had this phony intellectual look like the women who go to liberal, eastern schools. She reminded me of a bookish collie dog.

They asked me to read it again. So, I went through the whole goddamned speech again with them sitting there looking real grim like the whole world hung on this little piece-of-crap script. When I'd finished, the woman stands up and writes something on a slip of paper and hands it to the guys, and they read it and nod and then they get up and leave the room.

I went out in the hall and stood there and felt awkward and conspicuous and out of place and embarrassed like I used to when teachers would send me out of the room for screwing up. Kevin Costner came along, walking real jaunty and whistling and looking a lot more beat than in his movies.

I stood around in the hall for over an hour and finally got pissed and went back in and asked the collie dog what the hell was going on and she said, "Lunch." *Lunch!* Here I am hanging out in the hall like some nerd for over an hour because these people get an urge to go to lunch and bullshit and talk on cellular phones. Hollywood!

I grabbed up a pack of matches and set fire to the script and dumped it right in the middle of the collie dog's desk, and she started to scream at me and go bananas, and I gave her the finger and left.

Can you imagine these asshloes?

It is. But not as hard as farce.

—Edmund Gwenn (1875–1959), British actor, on his deathbed, in reply to the comment, "It must be very hard."

ERNIE

Ernie, a New York cab driver, opens interesting vistas.

After a while, you learn to read faces. You learn to spot people with bucks. It's like they've got "tips" written all over 'em. Every now an' then, though, you miss. Like here just the other day: I pick up this guy wearing a homburg out front of the U.N. building, and I figure him for like a big tip, you know. Hey! The sonofabitch goes and jumps outta the cab at a light and I get stiffed. I happens. But you usually can spot the turkeys.

I drive ten hours a day. A helluva long time to sit on your tush. My average speed is fifteen miles an hour. You don't make time in Manhattan. There are over 900,000 vehicles on the island during peak business hours. It gets crazy, let me tell you. When it gets too much, I pull into the park and meditate. I guess you might call me a Zen driver. After a few minutes, after I get myself together, I'm ready for the war again.

It's not a bad job, although sometimes I think maybe I shoulda gone on to college like my father wanted. He never got an education and he wanted us kids to. He was a cabbie, too, for over forty years. Both of my brothers went on to school. Abe, my older brother, he went to Columbia and became a lawyer with an oak-paneled office on Seventh Avenue. Stan, my kid brother, a super brain, went to Syracuse and came out a shrink with degrees up the wazoo.

Last year, Abe keeled over from a massive heart attack after going through a class-action suit against Con Ed, and Stanley is a certifiable loony with a zillion twitches from talking to sickos all day long. The way I look at it is, I may not have an education and a fancy-schmancy office, but at least I'm still healthy and my mind's not frozen yogurt.

And I make a good living and I get to meet some real interesting people, too. Hey, I could tell you some stories, pal, that would bend your briefcase. I get all kinds in this cab, lemme tell you. Everything from hookers to diplomats. The only difference is—the hookers always pay.

Theatre director: a person engaged by the management to conceal the fact that the players cannot act.

—James Agate (1877–1947), British theater critic

BASIL

Basil warns his girlfriend of the deleterious effects of jealousy.

I've told you a million times, I love you. I love you, I love you, I love you. Now—that's a million three.

Your jealousy's driving me up the wall, Jan. So, will you please give it a rest? Everything's okay, all right? You have nothing to worry about here. Just because I stopped to talk to the woman doesn't mean we have something going. Hell, I don't even know the person. Besides, it's real hard to get past her without saying something. After all, she *is* the checker. And her saying, "Green beans, seventy-nine cents" is hardly a come-on. And the same with that lady at the laundromat. She must have been seventy-five with whiskers growing out of her ears. C'mon now, be realistic. And the girl who delivers our mail with the moustache and thunder-thighs is definitely not my type. Will you please back off?

You're making me crazy with all this over-reacting. Like when I danced with Doris Robinson at the Christmas party. Don't you think spitting in her egg nog was a little heavy? I think maybe your insane jealousy stems from your childhood, from improper potty training. You know, Jan, maybe you should see a shrink, or something. I don't know. But I know one thing for sure: The jealousy's got to stop before it stops us.

GARY B.

Gary B. informs bar patrons of the benefits of a free-floating existence.

(*ENTERING with a flair.*) Howdy, everbody!

Set 'em up, barkeep, set 'em all around up on Gary B., the good-time man. And don't go pourin' none a that there cheap well crap, neither, 'cause I got me a coupla bucks in my pocket that's just scramblin' to get out.

I did me a little paper-hanging job yesterday; slapped on a little flower pattern for a rich bitch over in Bev Hills. I soaked 'er good for it, too, you're damned right I did, charged 'er plenty.

(*A little poem.*) When Gary B. works/He works for prime/ Not for a nickel/Not for a dime.

And when I got it, friends, when I got it, I spend it, I spread it around. What the hell's it all worth if you don't enjoy it? A person's gotta play it loosey-goosey with life and kick back and enjoy and take advantage of the fly speck of time he's got on this here planet. There's only one way to live this here life and that's at high RPM.

Some people think Gary B.'s a little down on the dipstick. If ya know what I mean. Think there's grit in my transmission. Well, so what! Hell, if they think my tires are a little low, they should take a good look at themselves sometime. Hell, I'm the sanest person I know. An' you know why? Because I live my life all-out crazy every single minute of every single day. If that's insanity, well then, friends, get me the suit with buckles in the back, 'cause I'm Grape Nuts.

(*Pulling a great wad of cash from his pocket.*) See this here little giraffe choker? Over two thousand bucks. All for slappin' a little paper on plaster. And you think I'm gonna go out and do something silly with it like slap it in a bank, or something? No way. I'm gonna put me this here wad to the torch of living, burn it up on friendship and women and song. Then, when it's history, I'll go out and pick me up another job.

One job at a time. No sense in overdoing, I always say. If a man works too much, it'll get in his blood and stain 'is soul. Knew this fellow one time who worked eighteen hours a day and wouldn't spend a dime. He hit the wall when he was just forty. When they did an autopsy on the poor bastard, they found out his heart was all clogged up with dollar signs. (*He begins to EXIT.*)

See ya 'round, suckers.

Why did I write? Because I found life unsatisfactory.

—Tennessee Williams (Thomas Lanier Williams, 1911–1983)

In music, the punctuation is absolutely strict, the bars and the rests are absolutely defined. But our punctuation cannot be quite strict, because we have to relate to the audience. In other words, we are continually changing the score.

—Ralph Richardson (1902–1983)

I made a career of playing sons of bitches.

—Kirk Douglas (1916–   )

All my life I've been dogged by guilt because I feel there is this difference between the way I look and the way I feel inside.

—Robert Redford (1936–   )

MEN: DRAMA

STEVE

Steve speaks to his counselor regarding his disenchantment with football.

I've been playing football since I was in grade school and here I am still cracking heads in college.

I used to enjoy the game, you know. But today—today it's more than a game—it's do or die, win at all costs; it's big-time sports involving millions and prestige for the school and the state. Education be damned. Forget about education.

Do you realize we've got guys on the team who are barely literate? But you can bet on it that they're going to graduate because they're All-American. We've got this one guy who's in Home Economics. Is this bullshit here, or what? Four years to learn how to make pie crust. What a goddamned shame. What an educational disgrace! Because if these people don't get picked by the NFL, their future is screwed. They'll be out on the streets prepared for nothing. And do you know what? Nobody really gives a fuck.

And football's become so goddamned brutal. Even with the improved equipment and training methods. Because the guys playing today are so much bigger and faster and because the emphasis on winning is so goddamned great. You're told to go out there and bust heads, to do whatever it takes, understand? Yesterday I went over to visit Ronald Johnson. You know, the guy who got blitzed in the Auburn game? Man, I couldn't believe it. Here he is, this great-looking guy—six four, maybe two forty—here he is lying there paralyzed. Paralyzed! And for what? A football game? Hell, his life's over, finished.

People have become crazed about this sport: The fans, the writers, the coaches, the alumni—faculty. When you stop to think about it, it's sick, you know. The sports thing has gotten way out of hand.

I'm thinking about dropping out. Because right now I'm real disillusioned. I don't know what the hell to do. I think I should get out, but. . . . (*Pause.*) Hell—football's all I know.

O God, send me some good actors—cheap.

—Lilian Baylis (1874–1937), British theater owner and producer

WINSTON

A drunken ne'er-do-well unleashes his hostility toward his wife's father, a self-made industrialist. His diatribe is a manifestation of frustration and self-pity.

That's enough, goddammit! I'm sick and tired of hearing it, okay? Daddy this, Father that. Father, Father, Daddy, Daddy! Fuck 'im! He's an unfeeling, unbending sonofabitch who's hard as flint. He doesn't have a heart, the old bastard. He's bloodless as a statue. He doesn't give a good goddamn for anybody, for their feelings or opinions. Christ, if he did, if he had any compassion at all, he'd have disinherited you. That way, maybe, you might have had a chance. But no—the sonofabitch makes you wealthy, poisons you with wealth and security and position and respectability. This way you can carry on after he dies, this way he's assured of immortality. The crafty old bastard, he misses nothing, takes advantage of every fucking opportunity. There's an ulterior motive behind everything he does.

Him and his self-righteous sense of commitment and direction. Jesus Christ Almighty! "Commitment, direction, goals!" These are his bywords, the pillars of his petit bourgeois, industrialist philosophy. Hell, people like him with their obsessive fucking commitment and achievement are the ruination of mankind. (*He snaps to attention briskly.*)

To arms! Onward, in the name of achievement! Enlist, young man! Uncle Achievement wants (*He thrusts a finger forward.*) —YOU! (*He snaps back to attention.*) Are your attachés at the ready? Are your ballpoints bared and ready for action? (*He whips a ballpoint pen from his shirt pocket, sharply removes its cap, and thrusts it forward as a readied saber.*) Then—CHARGE! (*He races about wildly, slicing the air with his saber/ballpoint. During the remainder of the speech his frenzy escalates to fever pitch.*)

Take that! And that! Take that, individuality! Take that, independence! Take that, free-thinkers! Take that, poets of the world! (*Slashing madly.*) Death! Death to all rarefied thought! Death to sensitivity! Death, death, death! (*He feigns being wounded.*) Aggggggghhhhhhhhh! (*He falls back as if mortally inflicted.*) I've been hit! I've been hit! I've been run through by achievement! (*He bursts into a paroxysm of laughter as he moves to a stand holding liquor. He pours himself a healthy ration of whiskey, still chucking hysterically. Then he toasts himself.*)

Drink up, everybody. Here's to Winston McBride—loser; to Winston McBride—unbearable drunk; to Winston McBride—ne'er-do-well. Long live Winston McBride. Yeah! Winston McBride for president! (*He downs the drink lustily.*)

LITTLE STICKS

Little Sticks speaks scathingly, admonishing his listeners for living in the past, for not addressing the present and facing the future. He touches on the problem of alienation between parents and their children.

Willya shut the fuck up about the goddamned drum set? You talk like it's human, or something, like it was everything in the whole world, for crisesakes. T' hell with the drum set! What about Sticks? What about him and what's happening today, right now, and what he must be going through? What about his feelings sitting there in the middle of a city dump with half a mind? What about that? Fuck the set and jazz and all of it. Screw the past and the so-called good times that don't mean a crap to anybody or anything. Fuck yesterday and living between the pages of a scrapbook with faded pictures that keep you from facing up to what's going down now!

What about today? What about you, and what about me, Harold "Little Sticks" Miller, the guy who came in second to jazz and who's been living with his head up his ass because he's been too bitter to forgive? And what about Sticks? The poor bastard. Today he said something, he acted and talked to me through the drum set. It's the only way he could get things out of that World War III head of his; the way only a father could get into it about his son. Man, that's sad as hell. (*He turns, confronts Bobby, Birdie's father.*) Like you. When are you going to get something going with Birdie? When are you going to quit talking shit and quit saying "wow" every other sentence and get down to it? When are you going to give her a chance and wake up to the fact that she ain't Charlie Parker? (*Turning to Birdie.*)

And you, you gotta knock off the crap, too, Birdie, and do what the hell you wanna do. Now, where the hell is Sticks? Exactly where the hell is he?

An actor's a guy who, if you ain't talking about him, ain't listening.
—Marlon Brando (1924–)

CLIFF

Cliff, a casualty of Vietnam, speaks bitterly of the war.

It was night, and we couldn't see a damned thing. They dropped a bunch of us up near the Mekong—from helicopters. Black as hell, it was, black as hell. We fell into mud up to our waists, and some of the guys got stuck and couldn't move and were helpless and the Cong blew the piss out of 'em. You ever see anybody get blown away? Like forget it, man—it's the lowest.

Then all hell broke loose, like in the middle of a thunderstorm. The ground shook and puffs of fire lit up the fields like they were taking pictures with giant flash bulbs. I move off into a clump of trees and unhook my chute and fold it up and Freddy and I —Freddy was my best buddy—then Freddy and I eased across a rice paddy toward Charlie, who was holding a lean-to village that wasn't worth losing a fly over. Then, alluva sudden, kaboom! This mine goes off and turns Freddy into instant hamburger just like that, and I go flying through the air like a fucking frisbee. The next thing I remember, I wake up in a chopper with a hunk a gristle in my sleeve.

The whole damn thing was a no-win war from the start. Fucking Kennedy and Johnson and Nixon—they were outta their minds for sending guys over there. Over fifty-five grand died for those assholes. Over fifty-five grand, Bobby, just think of it.

ROSS

Ross pours out his feelings of disdain for a non-feeling parent-age.

So what! So, the old man is dying? So, what's it have to do with me? You can go on back and wallow and blubber if you want to—not me. I don't want anything to do with the bastards! They're not my family, not the way they treated me. And you? For crisesakes, Jerry, don't you have any pride? They cut off your balls, those people. Hell, they damned near ruined us both. T' hell with the old man.

Where was he when I freaked out and they hauled me off to the mental hospital, huh? He was in Europe somewhere, too busy to come home, too involved with making bucks—that bastard. And Mom? Hell, she didn't give a fuck, either. All she was worried about was how me snapping out would make her look in the community, to the face-lifted bitches she hangs out with at the club. Hell, nobody raised a finger. *Nobody* ! And do you know why? Because they just didn't give a damn!

What in the hell ever happened to caring, Jer? Whatever happened to caring and decency and love and putting your flesh and blood before business and clubs and social horseshit? What ever happened to all that? Is this what it's all about here? That we were born to be rich fucking orphans? Is this it, Jerry? Is it? Or don't you care? Maybe you've gotten like the rest of them. Maybe you hung around too long. Maybe they got to you, too. Maybe some of their indifference rubbed off. Christ, I hope not.

So, he dies, so what! I don't have any feeling about it. He can die without me. He lived without me, now he can die the same way. He's a poor, sorry, rich sonofabitch. All of 'em are! They may have it in the bank, but they'll never have it where it really counts—in the heart.

You go on back if you want. Go on back and grovel and wear your best suit and stand around and get the piss kicked out of your self-esteem. Not me, Jerry! No way!

Bogart's a helluva nice guy till 11:30 P.M.
After that, he thinks he's Bogart.

—Dave Chasen, restaurateur

DANNY

A college student has had it with PC.

It's gotten to the point where you can't say a goddamned thing. Everybody's gotten so fucking overprotective of their little hunk of turf, you know. I mean, the attitude of sensitivity out there is ridiculous. You've got to go around treading on eggshells. Shit, it seems like everybody has this ax to grind. They're all up to their sensitive little tushes in the political-correctness thing. I mean, Christ—I can't even write an honest criticism anymore. Like when I said that that fucking off-the-wall dance production they staged last weak had all the grace of dogs in heat, you'd thought I'd crapped in the instructor's leotards, or something. He went ballistic. Tried to get me kicked off the paper. He said I showed gross insensitivity. Hey, all I did was write the best review I could based on my experience and knowledge of theater and dance, that's all. And why do I have to be sensitive to do a bunch of undisciplined jerks gyrating without form, or structure. Maybe the guy was outraged because I called attention to the fact he's given up teaching basics in favor of inane self-indulgence. It's like the poetry they submit to us for publication. It's crap. Abstract crap they try to pass off as art: rambling, word-association babble that's supposed to be this—this *profound* social statement. I call it the *Ode to a Texaco Restroom School*. Ginsberg, Ferlinghetti, and the old North Beach crowd can rest easy.

Those people were true artists who studied their craft—and worked.

This school's become nothing but a haven for the three M's: The maladjusted, the maladroit, and the malcontent. And because of it, we're graduating a bunch of airheads because everyone's too busy being offended to get an education. We've degenerated into an institution of politically correct bullshit. We've got student-action committees, student-defense councils, student-grievance bodies up the ass. And they're supported by faculty. Guys who are so politically biased that the patterns in their tweed jackets all run to the left.

I don't know how much longer I'll be able to stay on the paper. I'm getting heat from all directions. I guess my tenure boils down to one, simple, galling fact: I can be entertainment editor as long as I avoid the truth.

MORE BOOKS from DRAMALINE
AVAILABLE from YOUR BOOKSELLER

A WOMAN SPEAKS: WOMEN FAMOUS, INFAMOUS and UNKNOWN, ed. Cosentino. $12.95.

BETH HENLEY: MONOLOGUES for WOMEN, Henley. *Crimes of the Heart,* others. $9.95.

CITY WOMEN, Smith. 20 powerful, urban monologues. Great audition pieces. $9.95.

CLASSIC MOUTH, ed. Cosentino. Speeches for kids from famous literature. $8.95.

COLD READING and HOW to BE GOOD at IT. Hoffman. $12.95.

DIALECT MONOLOGUES, Karshner/Stern. 13 essential dialects applied to contemporary monologues. Book and cassette tape. $19.95.

DIALECT MONOLOGUES, VOL. II, Karshner/Stern. 14 more important dialects. Farsi, Afrikaans, Asian Indian, etc. Book and cassette tape. $19.95.

DIALECT MONOLOGUES—CD VERSION, Karshner/Stern. $22.95.

DIALECT MONOLOGUES VOL. II—CD VERSION, Karshner/Sterm. $22.95.

FITTING IN. Monologues for kids, Mauro. $8.95.

FOR WOMEN: MONOLOGUES THEY HAVEN'T HEARD, Pomerance. $9.95.

FOR WOMEN: MORE MONOS THEY HAVEN'T HEARD, Pomerance. $9.95.

FOR WOMEN: POCKET MONOLOGUES from SHAKESPEARE, Dotterer. $9.95

HIGH-SCHOOL MONOLOGUES THEY HAVEN'T HEARD, Karshner. $9.95.

KIDS' STUFF, Roddy. 30 great audition pieces for children. $9.95.

KNAVES, KNIGHTS, and KINGS, ed. Dotterer. Shakespeare's speeches for men. $8.95.

MINUTE MONOLOGUES for KIDS, Roddy. $9.95.

MODERN SCENES for WOMEN, Pomerance. Scenes for today's actresses. $8.95.

MONOLOGUES for KIDS, Roddy. 28 wonderful speeches for boys and girls. $9.95.

MONOLOGUES for TEENAGE GIRLS, Pomerance. $9.95.

MONOLOGUES for TEENAGERS, Karshner. Contemporary teen speeches. $9.95.

MONOLOGUES for WOMEN, Pomerance. $9.95.

MONOLOGUES from CHEKHOV, trans. Cartwright. $8.95.

MONOLOGUES from GEORGE BERNARD SHAW, ed. Michaels. $7.95.

MONOLOGUES from MOLIERE, trans. Dotterer. $9.95.

MONOLOGUES from OSCAR WILDE, ed. Michaels. $7.95.

MONOLOGUES from the CLASSICS, ed. Karshner. $8.95.

MONOLOGUES THEY HAVEN'T HEARD, Karshner. Speeches for men and women. $9.95.

MORE MONOLOGUES HAVEN'T HEARD, Karshner. More living-language speeches. $9.95.

MORE MONOLOGUES for KIDS, Roddy. More great speeches for boys and girls. $9.95.

MORE MONOLOGUES for TEENAGERS, Karshner. $9.95.

MORE MONOLOGUES for TEENAGE GIRLS, Pomerance. $9.95.

NEIL SIMON MONOLOGUES. From the plays of America's foremost playwright. $14.95.

NEIL SIMON SCENES. From the plays of America's foremost playwright. $14.95.

POCKET CLASSICS for WOMEN, ed. Pomerance. $9.95.

POCKET MONOLOGUES for MEN, Karshner. $9.95.

POCKET MONOLOGUES for WOMEN, Pomerance. 30 modern speeches. $9.95.

POCKET MONOLOGUES: WORKING-CLASS CHARACTERS for WOMEN, Pomerance. $8.95.

RED LICORICE, Tippit. 31 great scene-monologues for preteens. $9.95.

SCENES for KIDS, Roddy. 30 scenes for girls and boys. $9.95.

SCENES for TEENAGERS, Karshner. Scenes for today's teen boys and girls. $9.95.

SHAKESPEARE'S LADIES, ed. Dotterer. $9.95.

SHAKESPEARE'S MONOLOGUES for WOMEN, ed. Dotterer. $9.95.

SHAKESPEARE'S MONOLOGUES THEY HAVEN'T HEARD, ed. Dotterer. $9.95.

TEENAGE MOUTH, Karshner. Modern monologues for young men and women. $9.95.

VOICES. Speeches from the writings of famous women, ed. Cosentino. $9.95.

WHEN KIDS ACHIEVE, Mauro. Positive monologues for preteen boys and girls. $8.95.

WOMAN, Pomerance. Monologues for actresses. $8.95.

YOU SAID a MOUTHFUL, Karshner. Tongue twisters galore. $8.95.